NANCY WARREN

THE NEW WORLD OF AMATEUR RADIO

FRANKLIN WATTS
NEW YORK I LONDON I TORONTO I SYDNEY I 1986
A FIRST BOOK

Charts on pp. 20–21 reprinted from *The Computer FM Two-Way Radio Handbook* (#735), copyright 1974 by TAB Books Inc., Blue Ridge Summit, PA 17214.

Illustration on p. 28 adapted from *Britannica Junior Encyclopedia* by permission of Encyclopedia Britannica, Inc.

Illustrations by Vantage Art, Inc.

Photographs courtesy of: The Marconi Company Limited: p. 12; Larry Lisle/ARRL: p. 34; Radio Amateur Satellite Corporation: p. 50; Dave Bell Associates, Inc.: p. 54 (bottom); Steve Mervish: p. 62.

Library of Congress Cataloging in Publication Data

Ferrell, Nancy Warren.
The new world of amateur radio.

(A First book)
Bibliography: p.
Includes index.
Summary: Describes the variety of activities, organizations, and experiences available to the ham radio operator. Includes a brief history of radio and explains how radios work.
1. Amateur radio stations—Juvenile literature. [1. Amateur radio stations. 2. Radio] I. Title.
TK9956.F45 1986   621.3841′66   86-10991
ISBN 0-531-10219-X

CONTENTS

Introduction
7

CHAPTER ONE
Early Years with Radio
10

CHAPTER TWO
From Atoms to Airways
18

CHAPTER THREE
Getting Down to Basics
30

CHAPTER FOUR
Hams on the Go
39

CHAPTER FIVE
The Variety of Amateur Radio
45

CHAPTER SIX
The Service of Amateur Radio
57

Glossary
64

To Learn More About
Amateur Radio
68

Index
70

SPECIAL THANKS TO
MARWOOD HARRIS (KL7AW)
FOR HIS TIME, ENCOURAGEMENT,
AND KNOWLEDGE IN ASSURING
THE ACCURACY OF THIS BOOK.

I AM ALSO GRATEFUL
TO DEAN WILLIAMS,

MANY HELPFUL UNITED STATES
AND CANADIAN HAMS,

THE AMERICAN RADIO RELAY
LEAGUE, INC.,

AND THE JUNEAU AMATEUR
RADIO CLUB, JUNEAU, ALASKA.

N.W.F.

DEDICATED TO
ED

AND
TO HAMS
AROUND
THE WORLD

INTRODUCTION

Kodiak Island, Alaska, was peaceful that Friday. Rancher Louis Beaty was enjoying the view, overseeing his 200 head of cattle.

About midafternoon, strangely, the herd slowly turned and began plodding for higher ground. They had never done that before so early in the day. It was as if they sensed something unusual in the air. Puzzled, Beaty gazed around, but he found nothing disturbing in the blue sky, the gentle breeze, and the sleeping mountains.

Over two hours later, more than 20 miles (32 km) down toward the earth's core, rock masses shifted. Tons of earth rumbled and ground together, sending out shocks in all directions. Tremors reached the sea floor and exploded into the water.

At the earth's surface the crust heaved, rolling waves along the ground like swells on the ocean. In Anchorage, the quaking cracked water pipes, snapped electric wires, crumpled oil tanks, buckled train rails. In port cities, gigantic waves tore docks free, picked up and tossed boats far inland. People scurried for what safety they could find, but some were lost.

When the quaking finally eased, a stunned silence remained. Radio and television stations could not broadcast. Telephone lines were down. Many cities in Southcentral Alaska were without power, without heat, and without communications. How could people in the earthquake area let the rest of the state know that they urgently needed help?

This need was met by Alaskan *amateur* radio operators. Working with portable power, amateur voices flashed out to the rest of the state and called for planes, supplies, and medicines to be shipped to the stricken cities. They kept *wireless* messages humming back and forth through the long, dark night. In the days to follow, amateurs also sent messages to worried relatives in other states, keeping communications open until lines and power could be repaired.

Amateur radio operators—hams—were the faceless heroes during that disaster, as they were so many times in the past, and as they are today.

WHAT IS A HAM?

Just exactly what is a ham and where does the name come from?

The word *ham* has several meanings. To most people, it is a kind of meat. In the theatre, it is someone who overacts—"hams it up." In the world of communications, a ham is a licensed amateur radio operator. The place from which the ham sends and receives messages—in most cases a room in the home—is called a "ham shack."

No one knows for sure where the name "ham" comes from. Most likely it originated in the old days when an unskilled telegraph operator was called "ham-fisted" because he pounded the keys instead of pushing them down carefully. The name "ham" stuck, and is now the proud title connected with amateur radio.

Hams come from all walks of life—student, senator, engineer, convict, sailor, king, teacher, coal miner, store owner, nun, executive—you name it. They are male, female, from five years of age to ninety; they are all over the world.

Amateurs do not get paid for their work. They are much like Olympic athletes, who are amateurs and do not receive money for their performance. Amateurs do their jobs as a hobby, for fun, for the challenge, and for the service they perform. Few hobbies, however, can be fun and at the same time enable a person to make friends in other countries, talk in space, and save lives—all without leaving home. Every minute of every hour of every day, 365 days a year, radio amateurs around the world communicate with each other.

To be perfectly correct, you might say that amateur radio began a couple of thousand years ago when people became curious about electricity. However, the modern story could be brought forward to this century, to a windswept cliff overlooking the Atlantic Ocean.

CHAPTER ONE

EARLY YEARS
WITH RADIO

It was a blustery day in December of 1901, the sky wild with icy rain and wind. The place was Signal Hill, a high spot of land over-looking St. John's, Newfoundland, along the Canadian coast. On that rise, an aerial wire ran from the ground 600 feet (183 m) into the air. It was connected to a huge canvas kite which kept the wire aloft. The kite dipped and tugged at its holding line, threatening to tear free in the gale.

Inside a small building nearby, Guglielmo Marconi sat, a single earphone at one ear, listening. His work, his hopes were focused on this one point in time.

Suddenly, three faint clicks sounded through the noise of the earpiece.

Marconi bent his head, listening intently.

Again, the three clicks, spelling out the *Morse code* letter *s*, came through, faint, but there.

Marconi's spirits soared like the kite outside, for this moment in history marked the first wireless radio signal to cross the Atlantic Ocean from England to North America. It was an experiment—

reaching over 2,000 miles (3,220 km)—that changed communication throughout the world.

RADIO GETS ITS START

The hero of that moment, Italian-born Guglielmo Marconi, is called the "father of radio." Of course he did not build a radio from scratch. He took all the puzzle pieces of radio brought down through the centuries and made a workable picture of them.

Before radio, people passed messages as best they could. Soldiers built beacon fires on mountaintops or used mirrors to flash the sun's rays. Sailors at sea flew different colored sails. Although these methods were effective, the messages actually could not go very far—only within the sight of another human being. Imagine for a minute how a radio could have helped King Arthur, or Magellan, or even Joan of Arc.

Discoveries about electricity—the root of radio—were made as early as 600 B.C., about the same time in history that coins were first used as money. Because electricity could not be seen, it remained a mysterious force through the centuries. In the nineteenth century, however, several experimenters contributed important building blocks toward the development of radio. Englishman Michael Faraday, Scotsman James Clerk Maxwell, and German Heinrich Hertz were a few of the more prominent.

AMATEUR OPERATORS STEP IN

It might be truly said that all experiments in radio history up to Marconi were conducted by amateurs. Certainly such inventors were not paid for their work. Later in his life, Marconi patented his ideas and so received money, but he always liked to think of himself as an amateur.

Raising a kite and aerial at Signal Hall, St. John's, Newfoundland, in December 1901 for the first transatlantic wireless experiment. Marconi is on the extreme left.

Once Marconi used radio waves and sent them through the air without wires, the feat intrigued other people. This was especially so in the United States. Amateurs who had always had the experimenting fever dived into radio with spirit. Many were not interested in money; they just wanted to know how things worked. And they used anything at hand to build radio equipment—oatmeal boxes, bits of coal, copper tubing, milk bottles covered with tin foil.

Over several years to 1906, experimenters continued to find new ways. Englishman John Fleming, followed by American Lee

De Forest, developed a special radio tube. This item opened a path which allowed voice to be heard over the wireless.

In those early days particularly, radio was used by ships at sea. In one dramatic case, radio was used to bring a fleeing criminal to justice. Dr. Hawley Crippen had murdered his wife in London and fled aboard an ocean liner bound for Canada. British police discovered the ship he had escaped on. They sent a wireless message, and Canadian police were waiting to arrest Crippen when the liner arrived.

———————— CONFUSION ON THE AIRWAYS ————————

With the popularity of radio expanding, a problem developed. Soon the air became cluttered by commercial, military, and amateur radio messages signaling in all directions, and from many countries.

Perhaps the worst result of this airways jumble took place on April 14, 1912. On that night the liner *Titanic*, carrying over 2,200 people, struck an iceberg off the banks of Newfoundland. The wireless operator, Jack Phillips, and his assistant spent hours sending emergency signals, trying to attract passing ships for help.

"Come at once, we've struck a berg," tapped the message in Morse code, over and over.

But there was so much interference and confusion on the airways at the time, the message did not always get through. Several nearby ships, too, did not have their radios turned on or, for some other reason, did not hear. The ship *Carpathia* did eventually respond, picking up over 700 passengers from the water and from lifeboats. However, more could have been saved. As a result of this disaster, laws were passed which required twenty-four hour radio watch on certain classes of ships while at sea.

GOVERNMENT SETS UP RULES

Legislation for ships did not take care of all the radio problems. To bring order to the mixed-up airways, the United States Congress passed the Radio Act of 1912. One part of the law required that amateur radio operators be licensed. By the end of 1913, about 2,000 licenses had been issued to U.S. amateurs.

The act also said that amateur radio operators had to transmit at 200 meters (220 yd). That meant that when amateurs sent out messages over the air, they had to use radio *wavelengths* that were 200 meters long only. In a way, that action sort of pushed amateurs to the side. Because no one had broadcast at 200 meters or below before, radio experts thought that wavelength was worthless. To amateurs, however, that narrow broadcasting limit was just another challenge.

THE AMATEURS ORGANIZE

Though assigned to 200 meters only, amateur operators kept the Morse code clipping through the air. The hobby grew, and finally organized under the name the American Radio Relay League in 1914. Even today, the ARRL speaks for the largest number of amateur radio operators in North America.

When World War I threatened, amateurs banded together and offered their services in case of emergency. And then, because the enemy might pick up ham radio signals, the United States government closed all amateur stations for the duration of the war.

Nevertheless, amateurs were not idle. When the United States entered the war in 1917, hams were recruited into the services. With years of wireless experience, they were an immediately trained group. Who was better qualified to run the U.S. Signal

Corps than the 4,000 hams who were in military service? It was during the war years that radios were used in airplanes for the first time and earphones were perfected.

When the government lifted the ban on amateur radio after the war ended, hams were back in business. By then hams had several new inventions to work with. Edwin Armstrong, for instance, had developed an *amplification* system which sent signals over greater distances. These inventions helped hams make their own great discovery—the use of shortwaves.

———————— SHORTWAVES GO A LONG WAY ————————

Until the 1920s, very little experimentation had been done below the 200-meter wavelength. For that reason, the radio airways below that wavelength were considered useless. Messages could be sent for a few miles, but no one thought signals could be sent very far—certainly not great distances. Nevertheless, a few amateurs crept below 200 meters and experimented on the shorter wavelengths. And their signals flashed through successfully.

Making the 200-meter wavelength work was but one victory. The development of shortwaves was even better. Use of such short radio waves had to do with the atmosphere. Wireless operators had not yet discovered a key condition of the earth's atmosphere which opened up the world to radio. There had been hints and suspicions of this condition through the years, but it was the amateurs who were the pioneers of shortwave development.

About 50 to 250 miles (80–400 km) above the earth, are layers of electrified air—the *ionosphere*—which are activated by the sun. Radio waves of short lengths strike these gaseous layers much like a ball hitting a ceiling. They angle off those electric backboards and are reflected back to earth. They continue to bounce back and forth, over land and water, covering great distances. In this way they can be received by another, far-off radio before they become too weak to be detected.

In 1923, people did not fully understand this atmospheric condition. But it was then that three amateurs—Delay, Reinartz, and Schnell—using the shorter wavelength of 100 meters (110 yd), sent a signal from the United States across the Atlantic Ocean. After that, shortwave use blossomed.

With a discovery as important as shortwave, the government opened shortwave *bands*, or *channels*, to amateur work. If the usefulness of amateur radio had not been appreciated before this, certainly its experiments were then. And America's 16,000 hams—a 1929 figure—made full use of the privilege. They found the open airways exciting and challenging. Only four years later, ham radio ranks had exploded to over 41,000 in number.

—————— KEEPING ORDER ON THE AIRWAYS ——————

Commercial radio broadcasting began in the 1920s, too. In fact, an amateur, Frank Conrad of Pittsburgh, was one of the first to set up a commercial station. Radio caught on fast. At the beginning of 1922 there were twenty-eight stations; by the end of the same year, there were 570.

It became evident early on, as radio expanded throughout the world, that some rules had to be made. Otherwise the air, and space, too, would be a hodgepodge of sound. In 1932, world telegraph and radiotelegraph agencies combined into the International Telecommunications Union. This agency meets at World Administrative Radio Conferences with other nations, and helps assign *frequencies* in the radio *spectrum*. They also set up other regulations as needed. In the United States today, it is the Federal Communications Commission which makes sure world and national rules are followed in America. Currently there are about 1.5 million amateurs who signal on the airways around the globe.

Though Guglielmo Marconi was but one of many people who developed radio, he is still called its "father." And when he died in 1937, most of the world paid him honor. One day at 6:00 p.m., many countries went off the air for two minutes. During that time, no wireless messages were received or sent. It was a short moment in history to honor a man who had contributed so much to humankind.

But to fully realize Marconi's achievements, it is necessary to understand what radio waves are. To do that, the mind must picture something so small that billions of them would not weigh as much as a feather. That "something" is an *electron.*

CHAPTER TWO

FROM ATOMS
TO AIRWAYS

Many curious people through the ages found out about electricity and radio. Only now do humans understand some of their workings. However, there are still mysteries to be solved.

To understand how radio works, it is best to see how radio waves fit into the life of our universe.

THE RESTLESS ELECTRON

Everything in the world—people, water, stones, metals, air—is made up of *atoms*. Atoms are units of matter so tiny that no one has ever seen them. Yet scientists agree that atoms contain *protons* (positive particles) and electrons (negative particles) which react with each other like little magnets. The source of their power comes from our greatest energy giver, the sun. Electrons are lighter than protons and move around more easily. Atoms, with their lively electrons, are restless things.

Electrons are not much good, however, hovering around. They need an energy push to make them work, much like a swing needs a push to start it going. In your mind, picture standing dominoes when the first one is tipped to fall on the next and starts a chain reaction going. Electrons in motion, doing work, is another name for electricity. Once started, electrons flow along through the air or through matter much as a current of water in a river. But you cannot see electricity, which sometimes makes it hard to understand. It is around us, however. Try brushing your hair in a dark room on a dry day and watch the sparks crackle.

Electric currents are helped to move through space by magnetism. You have probably seen how ends of magnets pull or push each other. Electricity and magnetism are related and can produce each other. They can work in different ways. In radio, they produce *electromagnetic waves*.

There are many kinds of electromagnetic waves. Photography uses light rays, cooking uses infrared rays, medicine uses X rays. All the rays doing those jobs are very tiny waves being made so many times (so frequently) in one second that they are hard to measure. Microwaves and radio waves, which carry television and radio broadcasts, do not occur as many times in one second as other electromagnetic waves. They are therefore considered lower in frequency. Because of their lower frequency, radio waves are said to have a low place on the electromagnetic spectrum. Still, radio waves travel faster than our minds can even imagine.

————————————— MAKING WAVES —————————————

Radio waves look something like ocean waves. But the best way to see wave action itself is by the old pebble-in-the-pond method. Drop a rock in water and the rock pushes down the water where it enters. At almost the same time, the push forces the water nearest it to *crest* into a wave which in turn pushes the water next to it down into a *trough*, and so forth. The water itself does not go

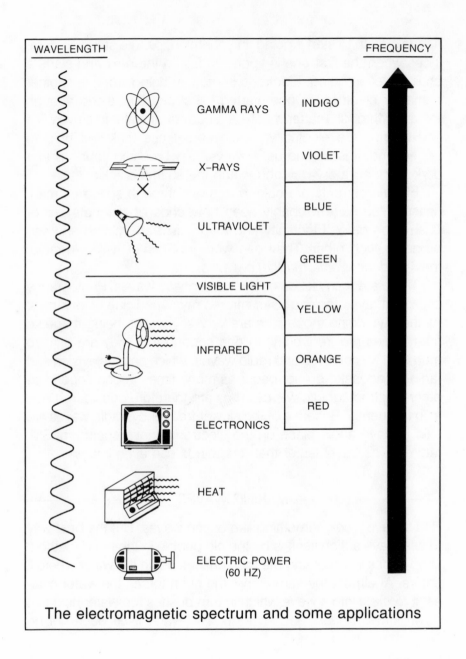

WAVELENGTH

FREQUENCY

GAMMA RAYS

X-RAYS

ULTRAVIOLET

VISIBLE LIGHT

INFRARED

ELECTRONICS

HEAT

ELECTRIC POWER
(60 HZ)

INDIGO

VIOLET

BLUE

GREEN

YELLOW

ORANGE

RED

The electromagnetic spectrum and some applications

WAVE LENGTH	BAND		USES	
	EXTREMELY HIGH FREQUENCIES: (30–300 GHz, 10–1 mm)		RADAR	
	SUPERHIGH FREQUENCIES (3–30 GHz, 10–1 cm)		MICROWAVE RELAYS, RADAR	
	ULTRAHIGH FREQUENCIES (300–3000 MHz, 1–.01 m)		TV CHANNEL 14–83. AIR CRAFT NAVIGATION AND DISTANCE MEASURING EQUIPMENT. MICROWAVE OVENS	
	VERY HIGH FREQUENCIES (30–300 MHz, 10–1 m)		TV CHANNELS 2–13. FM BROADCASTING: TAXI, POLICE, AND OTHER TWO-WAY RADIO COMMUNI-CATIONS.	
	HIGH FREQUENCIES (3–30 MHz, 100–10 m)		INTERNATIONAL SHORT WAVE BROADCASTING. AMATEUR RADIO. CB RADIO.	
	MEDIUM FREQUENCIES (300–3000 kHz, 100–1000 m)		AM BROADCASTING POLICE, SHIP, AND AVIATION COMMUNI-CATIONS.	
	LOW FREQUENCIES (30–300 kHz, 10–1 km)		SHIP COMMUNICATION AND NAVIGATION	
	VERY LOW FREQUENCIES (3–30 kHz, 100–10 km)	transmitter receiver	LONG-DISTANCE STATION-TO-STATION COMMUNICATIONS	

The radio–frequency spectrum, its divisions, and its uses

anywhere. A bigger rock causes bigger waves whose crests are higher. Eventually the wave flattens out again as it loses energy.

A radio wave is similar, but it goes in all directions like inside air pushing a balloon open. Radio waves sent in all directions allow many people to hear the same broadcast at the same time. Such waves can be different sizes or different frequencies, but they all travel at the same speed. Like the water wave, unless the radio wave is caught and used, it will eventually lose its energy push and fade away.

One entire up-and-down motion of a wave is called a *cycle*. The distance traveled in one complete cycle is the wavelength. Just as a tick of a clock tells the frequency of a second, so do cycles measure the frequency of a radio wave in one second. Since the number of radio cycles is so great when working, larger numbers are applied to the word *cycle* so everyone can understand the same meaning. *Kilocycles* are 1,000 cycles, and *megacycles* are 1,000,000 cycles. Another name for a radio cycle is a *hertz*, named after Heinrich Hertz. More recently, this term is used by ham operators. There are kilohertz (kHz) and megahertz (MHz) too. Check the face of a radio in your home, and you will see the letters there.

SOUND HITCHES A RIDE

In order for radio waves to be useful, they must carry sound of some kind. Waves of sound that we hear are like radio waves in many ways. Both are invisible, both travel through air, and both need "equipment" to do their jobs. With sound, someone talks and the sound waves travel to your ear. There they enter, hit your eardrum, and start it beating. The sound is sent to your brain which decodes it into a message that your mind understands.

Radio waves travel very much like sound waves, but the equipment they use are *transmitters*, *receivers*, *antennas*, amplifiers, and other radio items.

There is one big difference between sound and radio waves. Sound waves poke along in their travels compared with their radio cousins. Sound might travel two city blocks—1,088 feet (332 m)—in one second, but radio waves are superjets by comparison. A radio wave travels as fast as light, and in one second it travels 186,282 miles (299,914 km). That's like saying the word "hello" and by the time you have it out of your mouth, a radio wave has traveled around the world *more than seven times.* In one second! It took the fastest Concorde jet more than three hours to fly from Paris to New York, not to mention around the world, even one time.

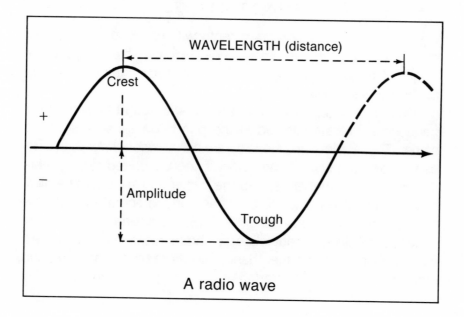

A radio wave

With such a difference in how fast sound and radio waves move, you might wonder how sound can be made to go faster. Electricity, however, makes things easier. With special equipment, sound waves can be changed to electromagnetic waves and be carried along at incredible speeds. When these waves reach their destination, special equipment changes electric waves back into sound waves so they can be understood as voices or music.

Basically, that is how radio works. Radio waves would not be much use if they did not carry a message of some kind. So, in order for a sound or voice wave to be carried through air, it must be matched to a radio wave which becomes the carrier wave. In other words, sound is converted to an electrical signal which *modulates*, or adjusts, the radio carrier wave. There are two ways of doing this.

MIXING THE WAVES

With the use of tubes or more recently with *transistors*, voice energy is converted into electrical audio signals which change the height of a radio wave (*amplitude*). AM radio stations use this method of transmission.

During early days of voice radio, it was found that the voice frequencies were contained in the bands on either side of the carrier. These added frequencies are called *sidebands*. Both sidebands carry the same information. It soon occurred to engineers that one of the sidebands, and the carrier as well, could be eliminated. The voice would still be carried on the one sideband. This new method of transmission—single sideband—has almost replaced amplitude modulation in communications. Using SSB, there is more room on the "band," so more hams can send and receive signals without interference.

The other way sound, in the form of an electrical audio signal, can hitch a ride on a radio wave is by changing the wave frequency. The radio waves stay at the same height, but they are forced to pack together or spread apart depending on the voice signals being used. When the carrier wave changes frequency at the voice rate, we call this frequency modulation (FM). In either case, by matching voice signals with radio waves, sound can jet along as a radio wave.

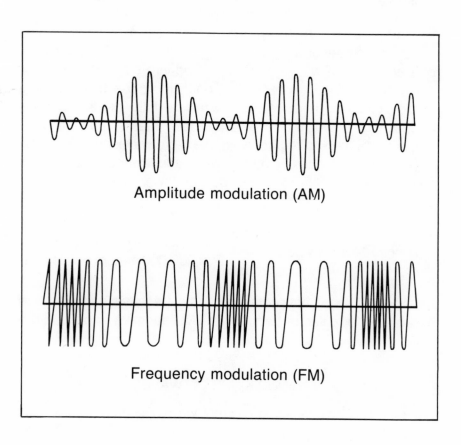

Amplitude modulation (AM)

Frequency modulation (FM)

FREQUENCY: HOW OFTEN
THE WAVES ARE MADE

Frequency is the number of waves per second, and is measured in cycles, or hertz. The length of a wave is the distance between the crests (or the troughs) of two adjacent waves, and is measured in the metric system by meters. The shorter the wavelength and the higher the frequency, the more energy the wave has. When a ham operator speaks about his 2-meter *"handie-talkie,"* he is packing a portable radio which sends and receives messages on waves 2 meters in length, or just over 2 yards long.

Since one second is the basic time measure of radio waves, different kinds of waves can be packed into that second. If you could draw a line of a basketball bouncing close to the floor, it would hit the wood many times in a minute. If the ball is pushed to bounce high, it would bounce only a few times in the same minute. In radio, the shorter the wave, the more waves there must be to fill that one second; a longer wave needs fewer cycles to fill the same second—the frequency would be lower. Scientists say it in a formula:

$$\text{frequency} \times \text{wavelength} \; \substack{\text{always} \\ = \\ \text{equals}} \; \substack{186{,}282 \text{ miles per second, or} \\ 300{,}000{,}000 \text{ meters per second}}$$

Most people do not have to use formulas, because their radios are already set for different frequencies. All they have to do is turn a dial.

VARIOUS KINDS OF WAVES

Different radio waves act in different ways. Because of this, they are used in special jobs. Very long wavelengths—some 20 miles

(32 km) from one crest to the next—are called ground waves. They are low in frequency and follow the curve of the earth. Air and ship navigation aids use such waves.

Shorter wavelengths (about 3 to 55 yards [2.7–50 m] long) are sent skyward and reflect from the ionosphere, traveling great distances over land and water. International traffic operators and hams signal with shortwaves.

Very short wavelengths (much less than an inch) crest many times in their one-second travels. They are called "line of sight" waves. If they are directed skyward, they pass though the ionosphere. Satellites use such waves. If the same waves are spread horizontally along the earth, they travel only as far as the eye can see, and are soon lost off the curve of the earth. Such waves need relay stations to catch and send their messages. TV stations use very-high-frequency signals.

ANTENNAS: THE PITCHERS AND CATCHERS OF RADIO

No matter what kind of wave, it needs an energy push to get started. In order to beam out or catch radio waves, an antenna is necessary. Otherwise, there would be a grab bag of waves in space, and no one would be able to zero in on one particular frequency.

Just as male mosquitoes use their "feelers," or antennas, to hear female mosquitoes, so are radio antennas used to send or receive radio signals. Perhaps you have seen the whiplike rods on cars, or the large dishlike reflecting antennas used for TV. The antenna beams out the radio waves in all directions, or in a special direction. The waves radiate through space with voice, video, or code information. A signal is also caught by an antenna, often the same one that sends a message.

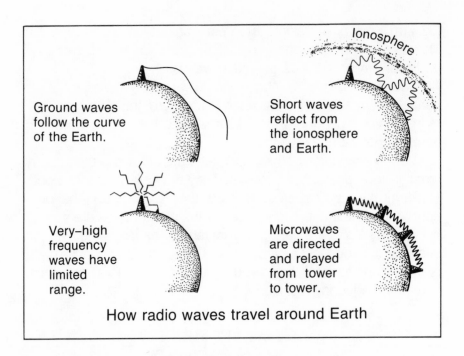

Ground waves follow the curve of the Earth.

Short waves reflect from the ionosphere and Earth.

Ionosphere

Very–high frequency waves have limited range.

Microwaves are directed and relayed from tower to tower.

How radio waves travel around Earth

The size and design of the antenna depend on the frequencies the amateur wants to send and receive. There is a mathematical relationship between the size of the radio wave being sent and the size of the antenna. That is why there are so many different types of antennas. Some antennas are so large and complicated, neighbors complain because the rods and towers are eyesores.

Most hams have antennas on their roofs. In order to avoid too much noise and interference, the antennas are placed as high as possible. Experienced hams like to say, "If your antenna didn't blow down last winter, it was not high enough." Most antennas can be turned around in place to position them where the signal is strongest.

Antennas can be constructed to direct radio waves, too; these are called directional antennas. If you have watered a lawn with a hose, you know the nozzle can be turned for a light spray fanning out broadly, or it can be turned to a straighter, stronger, more direct stream. Antennas can be designed to act the same way. Very-high-frequency waves flash out from a signal almost in a straight line, and are soon lost off the curve of the earth. Therefore they cannot go very far. Relay stations can be placed within sight of each other, however, and the beams can be directed by the antenna to shoot from one relay station to another.

Directional antennas can also be used with satellites in space. Since areas of space are becoming crowded, narrowing and directing a radio beam cuts down on interference with other orbiting satellites.

It is well to know of radio waves, frequencies, and antennas and how they work. But it does not tell much about the business of becoming a ham. That, you will learn, is a very personal hobby.

CHAPTER THREE
GETTING DOWN TO BASICS

Most large and small towns in the United States have amateur radio clubs. If you, for instance, wanted to become a ham, you could use your public library to locate a club in your community. From there you could contact a member and join a beginner's class. Most hams are eager to help a newcomer get started.

Or you could write directly to the American Radio Relay League, Inc., 225 Main Street, Newington, Connecticut 06111. The League would send you the name of an amateur radio operator in your area. The ARRL also provides packets to school classes so that students can get a hands-on experience with ham radio. If it is a project your school class might like to do, your teacher could write the ARRL for information.

THE FIVE HAM LICENSES

Amateurs must be licensed to send messages on the air. This is one basic difference from citizens band (CB) radio operators, who do not. CB'ers are also limited as to the distance of their transmissions, and the channels they use. Transmitting on citizens band radio is a handy way to learn about radio. In fact, a good number of CB'ers eventually find their way into the ham hobby.

In amateur radio, there are five types of licenses (sometimes called "tickets"). Each one is more advanced. It is not necessary to start with the first, or "Novice," license. The person who has the knowledge and skill to take any exam and pass has earned that license. One thirteen-year-old boy took the highest class exam the first time and passed. This is not usual, but it can be done.

Listed, the licenses are: 1. Novice, 2. Technician, 3. General, 4. Advanced, and 5. Amateur Extra.

"Novice" is the beginning class of license. Even if the only experience you have had with electricity is plugging a lamp into a wall socket, it is enough. But to earn a Novice license, you would have to learn a few basic facts.

A beginner must be able to send and receive five words a minute by international Morse code, plus answer a few written questions. The ARRL operates its own radio station whose call sign is W1AW. It sends out practice sessions in code on short-wave for newcomers. The organization also has tapes for sale. Practice records and tapes can be purchased from radio stores, and some hams loan their tapes. Like learning any hobby or sport, practice is the key.

If code seems like it would be hard to learn, think of Guy Mitchell who passed the Novice exam at the age of five. Of course his parents helped, but he worked hard and kept at it. Senator Barry Goldwater of Arizona, an amateur radio operator since the age of thirteen, suggests that young boys and girls who would like to earn their ham licenses "get with it and stay with it, study hard, and they can do it."

The written section of the test has to do with Federal Communications Commission rules, beginning practices, and a little radio theory. The whole test can be handled by another amateur of "General" class or above. The completed test is sent to the FCC by mail.

Once the FCC has issued a Novice license, the ham is on the way. At the present time, a new ham may use only international Morse code over the air, and only on certain frequencies. However, this rule could change. In the future there is a possibility that Novice hams may have voice privileges. A beginning license lasts for ten years and can be renewed before the time runs out. There is no cost for the license.

The second license—the "Technician"—requires the same five-words-per-minute speed for the code, but the written test is a bit harder. Questions deal more with radio theory, regulations, and operating. Technicians are allowed code and voice privileges over the air. Just think of turning on the ham rig and, for the first time, communicating over the radio with someone in another state.

Of course, do not choose a night like the one Tom Giugliano of Brooklyn, New York, chose after he jumped from a "Novice" to a "General" license. The time for his first voice contact over the ham set was a summer evening in July, and Tom's radio was hooked up to his house electric current. Warming up his rig, he felt very excited. It was the first time he had ever used a microphone over the air. Before long, he made radio contact with a friend. In the middle of his conversation the house suddenly went dark and the radio went dead.

Tom's parents called to him. They thought he might have blown some fuses because he had not loaded up properly. But it was not Tom's fault, and it was not even Brooklyn's fault. It just happened to be the night of the big blackout in New York—the blackout that left nine million New Yorkers without electricity.

The "General" license is the most popular. In that class, both voice and code can be used, along with most ham frequencies.

Requirements are a bit harder—thirteen words of code per minute—but the written test is the same as for Technician.

The next, the "Advanced" license, still requires the thirteen-word code speed, but has a harder written test. Most ham frequency bands as well as slow-scan TV can be worked by Advanced hams.

The "Amateur Extra," the most advanced license, holds the ultimate privileges for hams. The exam requires a twenty-words-per-minute code speed and a difficult written test. Such a test includes knowledge of computers and microcomputers. All ham bands are open to "Extra" operators, plus a few experimental bands that other hams cannot use.

SETTING UP A STATION

Gearing up an actual station requires very little. All you need basically is a transmitter, a receiver, and an antenna. One ham made a low-power transmitter in a tuna fish can. It does not take expensive equipment or super power to reach distant locations. Everything could easily fit on a small table or desk.

You can buy the gear directly from a radio store. The rig could cost something like a stereo set or a CB radio—maybe under three hundred dollars.

Or you can scrounge parts and keep expenses to a minimum. Making your own rig—with the help of another ham, an "Elmer"—gives you more information about how the parts work.

Some companies manufacture kits which are easy to put together. They are usually less expensive than completed gear and are fairly easy to assemble. No special technical knowledge is necessary.

Most hams set aside a room or a corner of their home for the ham shack. They rig an antenna of some kind on the roof or near the house to send and receive radio signals better.

When you become a ham, you are assigned a call sign all your own. You use this call sign on the air to identify yourself to other hams.

For example, after signaling "CQ, CQ," which is the call to anyone listening on the frequency, you would then give your own call sign to tell a potential contact who you are. A great number of operating hams do not even know the last names of their contacts—only their call signs. No one else can have the same call sign anywhere in the world.

The call sign tells about the person who owns it. The first letters indicate what country the amateur is from. Here are a few examples:

United States	— W, K, N, A	Japan	— JA, JR
Canada	— VE	Peru	— OA
England	— G	New Zealand	— ZL

Above: fifth-grade teacher Larry Lisle, of Rockford, Illinois, helps students become amateur radio operators. Here hams Kristine Schaefer, Gary Hopewell, and Lynn Holliday copy along while John Hernandez operates the classroom station. Below: Larry Lisle's Rockford, Illinois, fifth-graders learn what electronic components look like while getting a supply for transmitters and other projects. Here hams Chris Upchurch and Jim Alsbury salvage parts from an old TV.

ALBUQUERQUE ACADEMY
MIDDLE SCHOOL

Once you are assigned a call sign and keep it current, it is yours for life—no matter where you might move in America. Because hams are proud of their hobby, many arrange for car license plates with their call sign on it. If necessary, such plates alert government officials at the scene of an emergency that a ham is on hand to help with communications.

——————— QSL's: COLLECTING CARDS ———————

QSL cards are personal items of amateur radio as well as being fun. When hams send out a CQ (a general request for anyone to answer), they never know who will respond, or from where. It could be someone in another state, or even another country. When two hams make contact on the air for the first time, they log in, or keep a record of the contact, and usually exchange QSL cards. Such cards are the size of postcards and have the call sign on one side, and information about the contact on the other—the date, frequency, and time. Hams collect these and often cover their ham shack walls with the cards. They call it "wallpaper."

A ham can earn other awards to display, too. The ARRL gives certificates to hams contacting certain locations. There is the WAS (Worked All States) certificate which means the ham has had radio contact with at least one ham in each state. A DXCC (DX Century Club) certificate means a ham has worked 100 countries, and it is a much-sought-after award. Another award is the WAC (Worked All Continents).

Not only is an award given for completing contacts as mentioned above, but further awards can be earned through using different types of ham equipment or methods. WAS awards can be earned through radiotelephone ("phone"), or voice, or international Morse code, or perhaps on a given frequency band. Since hams have their own orbiting satellite (OSCAR), they can earn a WAS certificate by contacting all states through the satellite. Hams even have a Rag Chewers certificate which requires a half hour on-the-airways conversation with another ham. A ham can earn further awards by competing in contests with fellow amateurs.

─────────── THE PROBLEM OF LANGUAGE ───────────

People who are not amateur radio operators could easily ask the question, "How do hams talk to other hams who don't speak the same language—especially when ham signals reach to other countries? Even international Morse code has an alphabet, and not all alphabets are the same throughout the world."

English is spoken in many parts of the globe, which solves some of the problem. Amateurs use a code which helps with the rest of the problem. The system is called the Q code.

Many years ago when radio first began, people immediately discovered that language would be a problem. How, for example, could a radio operator on a French freighter traveling to New York, receive important weather information from an American operator on shore when they didn't speak the same language?

It was not long into radio when an early world radio convention adopted the Q signals, three-letter initials all beginning with *Q*. Though brief, the code covers enough of an idea to exchange information between hams of different languages. Each set of letters can be used as a question or an answer. A ham can use the signals in voice or code. A conversation might go something like this:

American	*Brazilian*
QRZ (Who is calling me?)	QRZ (You are being called by) Manuel Vargas.
QRQ (Shall I send faster?)	QRS (Send more slowly.)
QRG (Will you tell me my exact frequency?)	QRG (Your exact frequency is) . . .

By using Q codes, much of the language problem can be eliminated.

Within a country, amateurs are able to be of service to the public because they have linking radio systems already set up. Just as commercial radio companies maintain networks, so do amateurs. Groups of hams get together over the air on a regular basis because they have interests in common, and because they live in the same general area.

Dean Baker, for instance, is a member of the Wyoming Cowboy Net. Members of his group meet at a scheduled time most nights, just for the fun of it. This network, like many others, is an established linking system which is available in case of emergency. It is also a relay for passing messages anywhere in the world.

In addition, there are Maritime Mobile Nets called "Mickey Mouse Nets," which help people out on their boats. If someone has an accident and needs assistance or a doctor, hams find out the information and send for help. To name only a very few such groups, there are the Hamfesters Info Net in Illinois, the Moose Lake Repeater Net in Minnesota, and the Alberta Traffic Net in Canada.

Most amateurs stay at home and transmit from their ham shacks. Yet there are times when they get out and socialize with other hams. And there are a few who are not satisfied with airway "travel" alone. They want the excitement of actually traveling to other countries. Whether going mobile in a car, setting up a Field Day exercise, or flying to another country, amateurs are on the move.

CHAPTER FOUR

HAMS ON THE GO

The place was Navassa Island, a windswept dot in the Caribbean. The island is 1 mile by 2 miles (1.6 x 3 km) in size, with cliffs rising on all sides. No one lives on the island, but it qualifies as a separate "country" because it is over 225 miles (362 km) from its governing U.S. mainland.

Nine American hams traveled to Navassa to set up four radio stations so that other hams could make yet another "country" contact. With them, the amateurs brought antennas, generators, pipes, electrical equipment, water, and food—everything.

Once the stations were working and Navassa was for the first time "on the air," a pileup of voices called in asking for contact and a QSL card. The voices were eventually sorted, and the signals acknowledged.

For six days, twenty-four hours a day, the short transmissions shot back and forth. After the week was over, more than 33,500 hams had contacted the island—some from as far away as Australia.

The trip to Navassa was but one of the exciting DXpeditions arranged by adventurous hams. It is part of the fever of making a new contact, collecting yet another country of the more than three hundred nations around the globe.

DXing: LONG-DISTANCE HAM CONTACTS

DXing—long-distance hamming—produces a special breed of ham. Such an amateur is intent on one goal—contacting all the 318 "countries" of the world as recognized by the ARRL. Of course some locations do not have hams, let alone many people, like Navassa Island. A DXpedition travels to those remote spots, sets up a ham station, and provides the on-site contact for other hams around the world.

A well-known DXer who has been in the ham hobby for many years is Dave Bell of California. To newcomers joining amateur radio, Dave says, "Ham radio is not for everyone, but for some few special people, it is the adventure of a lifetime."

THE CHALLENGE OF LONG DISTANCE

Long-distance hams found out from the start that sky conditions played a part in their successes and failures. But they did not know how.

Earlier, mention was made of the ionosphere and its effects on radio waves. A little was said of the layers of gases which blanket the earth 50 to 250 miles (80–402 km) above it. These layers become electrically charged from the sun. A radio wave can be made to reflect off these layers and "skip" to a distant location, much like a motorized volleyball.

Nothing in the atmosphere stays the same, however. Many factors affect whether a radio signal gets through and where it

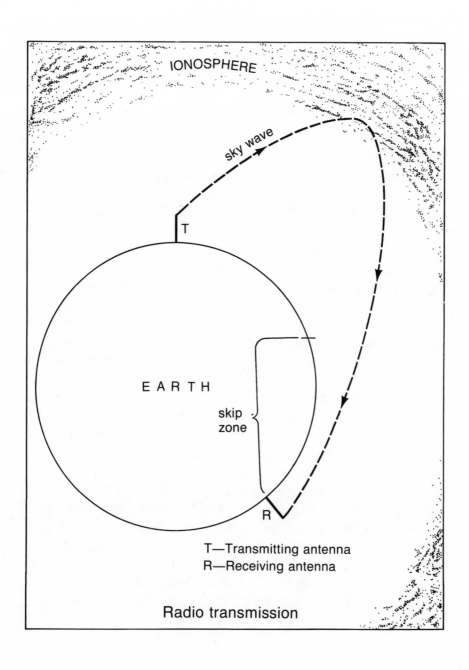

IONOSPHERE

sky wave

T

EARTH

skip
zone

R

T—Transmitting antenna
R—Receiving antenna

Radio transmission

ends up. The electrified layers become more fully charged during the day than at night. Seasons of the year make a difference. The angle and frequency of the signal are other factors. There is still much to be learned about radio wave behavior in the atmosphere—or what is called *propagation.*

Explosions on the sun (*sunspots*) also affect the ionosphere. Such explosions send out terrific charges of energy which eventually reach our atmosphere. Sunspot activity rises and falls over eleven-year cycles. During these periods, radio transmitting and receiving are also affected. When sunspot activities are high, radio propagation gets better. Even radio frequencies that were good for only short distances can be used for international contacts during high sunspot activity periods.

Another factor which affects the ionosphere—and hence radio waves—is *meteor scatter.* Though we cannot actually see them from earth, meteors from space continually enter our atmosphere. Because of friction as they shoot through, meteors burn up quickly. But as they do, a tail of dense electric particles is formed. Such a heavy electric funnel, or show, can cause a burst of reflected radio message to be heard. Normally the message might not get through. But the area electrified by the meteor particles allows the signal to be reflected. Some meteors that shoot into our atmosphere can keep a reflected message going for over a minute from long distances away.

Such differences as sunspots and meteors change the ionosphere all the time. For DXing, that is the challenge. A ham must find the right layer of ionosphere at the best time. A ham must also set the antenna correctly to send out a signal and have it skip to the correct—or to a new—location. Then the ham must adjust everything if the signal fails to follow through properly.

But it is not necessary to travel to foreign lands to DX. Some amateurs prefer to ham it up close to home while still moving around. These hams use a more down-to-earth form of transportation.

GOING MOBILE

Going mobile means just that—on-the-go with a ham set. With today's solid-state equipment, and receiver/transmitters combined into one *transceiver*, a ham station fits under the dashboard of a car. A number of amateurs install ham sets in their boats, and some have them in their airplanes.

The fun of going mobile is the surprises. From a fixed shack at home, a ham has a good idea of where the signals will go. In a mobile rig, the conditions change all the time, simply because the car ham radio is moving with the driver. Because of these changing conditions, there is a better possibility of contacting a new and distant location. One amateur, driving among the skyscrapers of New York City, contacted hams in Germany, England, and Morocco in one afternoon—all while inching his way through heavy city traffic.

OUT IN THE FIELD

For those hams who do not tramp to distant lands on DXpeditions, or do not have mobile units in their cars, amateur radio is still a social hobby. Besides talking on the air with other amateurs and going to monthly meetings, local clubs set aside at least one weekend in June to gather as a group in the field. Appropriately, the outing is called Field Day. It is a weekend period when hams all over the United States and Canada set up temporary radio shacks in their locations. The spot may be a park, a hill, a mountaintop, a lake—anyplace outside in the rough, away from their standard shack. They use tents or simple camping gear and transmit on portable power.

Field Day rules are simple. Hams must operate their radio sets with batteries or portable *generators.* The idea is to make as many radio contacts during a twenty-four-hour period as possible.

But Field Day serves a more serious purpose, too. It is a chance to test portable power which might be needed in case of a disaster. Should a local emergency occur and electric power be cut off, hams must be ready with portable power that can operate by itself. Such was the case during the Alaska earthquake, and is the case in so many disasters. So if the Field Day weather is bad, in a way, that is good. Wind and rain only test the equipment and the conditions better.

HAMFESTS

If they like, amateurs can get together through hamfests, too. They are informal conventions where hams make "eyeball" contact and meet some of the faces that go with the call numbers.

Rather than working radio at these events, they are more like equipment conventions. Manufacturers often bring the latest in ham gear. Because of this, it is a good place for newcomers to compare transceivers, antennas, and even computers and software. A hamfest provides a hands-on experience for the amateur. Such events are held on local, state, and national levels.

CHAPTER FIVE

THE VARIETY OF AMATEUR RADIO

Whether DXing to Rome, or just signaling across town, amateur radio is full of variety. Once into the hobby, each ham seems drawn to a certain side of amateur radio. And there are many—some that actually take messages out of this world.

—————— CONTINUOUS WAVE MESSAGES ——————

Morse code—a system of sending a signal over a wire—is older than radio. The code was used during the Civil War (1861–65) in railroad stations and telegraph offices. American Morse code was designed by Samuel Morse, and is slightly different from international Morse code, which was originally developed in Europe and is simpler to use. However, the idea is the same.

Hams often refer to international Morse code as continuous wave transmission (CW). With this method, a ham set generates a constant flow of radio wave energy, which is broken by the dots and dashes of the coded signal. Continuous wave transmission uses a very narrow space on the airways and requires little power.

In this day of easy voice messages, you might ask why hams need code at all. First, code is the simplest method for world use. It is inexpensive, too, which helps nations that might not have money to put into complicated, costly equipment. Also, in a pinch, when an important message must reach another destination, code does the job under all kinds of bad conditions. Code gets through. Skilled code users can sometimes even identify their friends by the way they tap out the signal. It's kind of like recognizing a voice.

Experimenters now are finding ways to use home computers along with radio equipment. A computer, for instance, can be programmed to act as a Morse keyer. Electrically, it can automatically space between the dots and dashes formed in CW. It also has a memory to store messages which can be later recalled. Some come with an electric voice which sounds like a robot.

THE OLD TELETYPE GOES MODERN: RTTY AND ASCII

In old movies, Western Union operators tapped out a message on what looked like a typewriter. The message would be sent and then typed out in capital letters on a tape at the other end. The tapes were then pasted on a Western Union message form.

A small group of amateur radio fans modified this machine for ham transmissions and use it to send radio messages today. It works much like the old teletype machine. In most machines, the motor is at rest until a typewriter key is pressed. Then the proper pulse character is formed and the motor comes to rest again before the next key is depressed. Machines are geared for different speeds, and some can make as many as a hundred words per minute if the operator can type that fast. The message is sent and then typed out on a tape or page at the receiving end so that a person does not have to be present. The typewriter at the sending station may also print a message coming in.

RTTY became a natural to use with computers which already had a keyboard. Computers use ASCII (American Standard Code for Information Interchange), the language of the terminal. Hams now use this code to talk from computer to computer. The system is fast replacing the old RTTY-style machines. Computers are not only faster and more efficient, but they are also quiet in contrast to the clacking of the old Western Union machines.

THE HANDIE-TALKIE (HT)

Perhaps most popular of ham equipment is the shoe-size, 2-meter (FM) "handie-talkie," which looks much like a single walkie-talkie. The hand-held set has a push-to-talk button which allows signals to either be sent or received one at a time, rather than overlapping. Battery operated, this solid-state transceiver uses a short antenna for both sending and receiving. The antenna, coiled and rubber-covered, is only 6 inches (15 cm) long and is often called a "rubber duckie."

The handie-talkie is a product of the computer age. It is composed of digital readouts and circuits, memory frequency channels, and automatic *scanners* which search the bands for live channels. Almost half of the U.S. hams now have 2-meter handie-talkies, some of which are nearly as small as a deck of cards.

If you stop for a minute, you could probably think of all kinds of activities where 2-meter radios would come in handy. They are used at parades, sports events, and walkathons, as well as for local emergencies, to mention a few. One young ham carried his handie-talkie on a touring vacation. In the summer of 1984, a fourteen-year-old ham sent messages by 2-meter radio while on a bicycle tour on the East Coast. With the help of a ham relay network, messages by the group were sent and then forwarded to families in such places as Chicago, Quebec, and even Tucson, Arizona.

But handie-talkies can be used for listening too. NBC news correspondent and executive Roy Neal remembers his time as a newsman at the Johnson Space Center in Houston in late 1983. Neal, an avid ham, had helped to set up an amateur broadcast from the space shuttle *Columbia*—the first time a ham broadcast was to be manned in orbit. Aboard the *Columbia* was ham astronaut Owen Garriott. As the shuttle overflew southern California, Roy Neal tuned in his handie-talkie and heard astronaut Garriott from space—some 1,500 miles (2,415 km) away!

BOOSTING THE SIGNAL: THE REPEATER

Because the handie-talkie works on line-of-sight wavelengths and very high frequencies, the signal does not travel long distances. A message can normally go as far as a person's vision. Two-meter operation, therefore, is often used with a *repeater* station.

Such a ham station is an unmanned, automatic receiver/transmitter/antenna unit which gives a power boost to the signals in the area. It is a boxlike affair which receives on one radio frequency and then automatically transmits the signal on a different frequency. To eliminate interference and to send for the longest distances possible, repeaters are placed high on the tops of buildings, on hills, or on mountain peaks, and usually transmit at higher power levels. There are few communities in the United States that are not within range of a repeater from some direction. Such communications make it enjoyable and convenient for the traveling ham.

A handy feature of most repeaters is called an *autopatch*. This is a process that allows an amateur on foot or in a car to connect up with the telephone company through the repeater. Since there is already a set of number keys on the face of the handie-talkie, a ham can make a phone call to anyone who has a telephone in the community. A repeater using an autopatch system can be costly for the local amateur radio club members.

OSCAR: MESSAGES SENT OUT OF THIS WORLD

Becoming an astronaut might be a goal of yours, one you could achieve after years of schooling and training. But right now, at whatever age you are, you could do satellite work as a novice amateur radio operator through *OSCAR*—the Orbiting Satellite Carrying Amateur Radio.

The first OSCAR was built by a few hams in California and was launched in December 1961. The Californians scrounged parts for the first satellite and ended up having to pay only sixty-two dollars in out-of-pocket expenses. The satellite was not sent by itself but hitched a ride on an Air Force military satellite, *Discovery 36.* For eighteen days *OSCAR 1* broadcast "Hi" by international Morse code to hams all over the world until its battery was used up. Even though it lasted less than three weeks, more than 5,000 hams in twenty-eight nations heard the signals.

Basically, the later *OSCAR* packages are actually radio repeaters. Instead of the repeater being placed on a hilltop, it is launched miles into the sky and is carried in a path which always circles the earth. The satellites have been designed so that they can be used with ordinary amateur equipment.

Contact is made with the satellite through CW or SSB from a ham shack. The signal is sent on one frequency (the *uplink*), is processed through the satellite like a *transponder*, and is sent to a desired location on another frequency (the *downlink*). It is interesting to note that a ham can hear his own signal on the downlink, as others hear it.

Since the beginning, each *OSCAR* has aided the advancement of amateur radio. In 1969, a Washington, D.C., group formed AMSAT (Radio Amateur Satellite Corporation), a nonprofit scientific organization. Through the years this group has worked with amateurs in other parts of the world so that several *OSCAR*s have actually been international projects. All the *OSCAR*s since *OSCAR 5* have been launched as side packages of NASA spacecraft. The Soviet Union, too, has sent up its own amateur radio satellites which are used by hams around the globe.

The ninth *OSCAR*, a United Kingdom/United States project launched in 1982, stands out, particularly, as a classroom aid. The ARRL and AMSAT provide, free of charge, educational materials that outline numerous classroom projects through the *OSCAR* satellite. Hams actually come into the classroom to demonstrate. There, prearranged satellite contact can be made with amateur stations in the United States and more than eighty other nations.

OSCAR 10, sent up in June of 1983, is one of the more advanced amateur projects. It was a joint effort of amateurs from West Germany, Hungary, Argentina, Japan, Canada, New Zealand, and the United States. Whereas the older *OSCAR*s rode low in the sky and allowed about two hours of contact a day, the newer satellites ride high in the sky and allow close to ten hours of contact for the same period. Instead of the 2,000-mile (3,220-km) contact with the old *OSCAR*s, the new ones receive and send from ten times that distance.

The OSCAR 10 *spacecraft in Germany being tested by a vibrating machine to assure it can survive the rigors of launching.*

Such distances are reached by using an *elliptical* (ovallike) orbit around the earth. The *apogee* (highest point) is over 23,000 miles (37,000 km) away. And because of this high repeating *OSCAR*, not only can hams talk for longer periods of time, but the satellite can signal to a larger area of the earth's surface. Antennas, too, need not be fancy. One ham made his antenna out of a special pipe and wires, plus a 3-foot (91-cm) square reflector of hardboard covered with ordinary tinfoil.

There are other advantages of the new, high-riding *OSCAR*s. Propagation, for instance, has little effect on the signals. Also, since *OSCAR*s are powered in part by solar panels, the sun helps keep the satellite alive. Microcomputers, too, are on board to control the craft's many systems. Besides providing an immediate call for help in case of disaster, the high *OSCAR*s also provide country linkup for "round table" discussions. Nations such as England, Japan, and the United States, for example, can discuss projects as if they were in the same room.

Zeroing in on a high *OSCAR* satellite in order for it to receive a signal can be done either by hand or by computer. By hand, an *OSCAR*-locator is used. This is simply a map overlay with markings that plot the movement of the *OSCAR*. Since orbital paths can be predicted, schedules can be figured ahead of time. Several amateur radio publications print such information. The computer approach needs a software program that gives details of exactly where to point an antenna.

In the future, amateurs hope to be part of a NASA shuttle which will eject an experimental amateur satellite system called *PACSAT* (packet radio satellite) into low orbit around the earth. *PACSAT* is a computer program that will allow amateurs to send electronic messages on uplink channels and have them stored in the spacecraft for later transmission to hams around the world. It will act somewhat like a flying post office. Such stations can be linked to any personal computer.

TELEVISION FOR THE AMATEUR: SLOW-SCAN (SSTV)

Since this book is about radio, you might wonder what a section on television is doing in it. After all, you cannot see invisible radio waves, but you can see television pictures.

By now, however, you know that radio and television are cousins. Even the commercial television you see in your home is not actually a picture sent over the airways to your set. It is instead a picture broken down to light, then converted to electricity, then to radio waves, and everything converted back again on your home TV set. A great deal of complicated equipment is used to bring these images to your home.

Amateurs have been experimenting with TV for over fifty years. By 1960, they were transmitting color TV signals. Regular commercial TV, however, takes up too much room on the airways. Because of this, amateurs are not allowed to use commercial TV channels. Amateur experimenters had to think of another way.

What hams came up with is called slow-scan television (SSTV). This mode is open to hams with a General class license or above. All that is needed for SSTV is a single sideband station, a TV monitor, and a camera. The camera is not even necessary if a tape recorder is available.

Amateur radio operator Cop Macdonald got the idea for slow-scan TV as long ago as the mid-1950s. He was a junior at the University of Kentucky when he read about a bank sending a person's signature over a telephone line. Because regular TV uses motion and needs sharp detail, it takes up so much space on the airways—like using 2,000 telephone lines for a picture. Cop Macdonald knew this. But here, Cop read, was a signature, an image, being sent over but one telephone wire. If that could be done, why not something else? The idea fascinated him. Through years of subsequent study and experimentation, slow-scan developed.

*Below: long-time ham Dave Bell
of California is known for his
DXpeditions—one, for instance,
to Macao, an island near China.
Right: Copthorne Macdonald of
Canada is one of the important
developers of slow-scan television for amateur radio.*

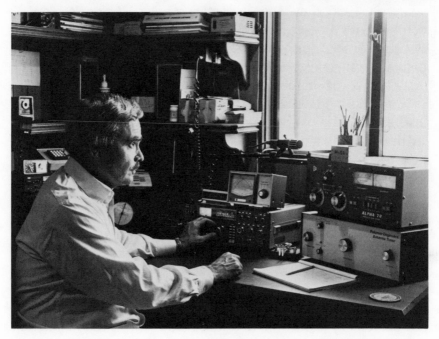

SSTV is not a motion picture, but more like a slide show. It uses sixteen "musical" tones which signify sixteen shades of gray, from black to white. A certain tone of light gray means a certain musical note. A picture as such cannot be sent over the air, but the musical tones can. The radio at one end codes the picture from a camera or tape recorder and sends it to another ham who has a radio to decode the notes back to grays and show it on a monitor.

Because SSTV uses only a little frequency bandwidth, the musical notes are sent in batches and appear on the screen from top to bottom in layers as they are decoded. It takes about eight seconds for a total picture to appear. In commercial television, thirty complete pictures are sent every second to preserve the illusion of movement.

Hams at either end of a contact use TV or computer monitors for screens. Regular cassette tapes can record and save the musical notes, and they can be played back as a picture later on.

Most of the pictures sent by SSTV are of the ham, his family, or his equipment. Magazines, newspapers, and slides are also sources of material. One ham, however, recalled receiving photographs from outer space. When NASA's *Voyager* space probe traveled close to the planet Jupiter in 1979, photographs were sent back to Earth. Amateurs involved with the *Voyager* project took time to rebroadcast the photographs on slow-scan for their TV ham friends.

FAST-SCAN TELEVISION (ATV)

A household TV channel uses 70 percent more radio spectrum than is available to amateurs in the total high-frequency and medium-frequency ranges combined. Hams, therefore, cannot use regular fast-scan TV on channels which interfere with commercial broadcasts. Because of this, amateurs are allowed only on ultra-high frequencies where there is more air space. Such room in the radio spectrum is mostly used for experimental purposes.

For those hams who do operate fast-scan on the ultra-high frequencies, they usually buy and modify standard TV equipment for that purpose.

WORKING FASCIMILE (FAX)

Related to SSTV is a system called *facsimile* (FAX). This method simply puts the SSTV picture, sent by a continuous radio wave carrier, on paper rather than a monitor. A Western Union–type machine is used with a drum which is covered with electrosensitive paper.

The system works like this. A document to be sent is wrapped on a drum. It is then scanned by a photoelectric cell which converts the lines to a radio carrier wave. The wave is sent over wire or radio. At the receiving end, the wave variations are converted to black and gray regions on the copy. A fine wire advances along a drum recording the signal—and making the image—as the message is received. In commercial offices, facsimiles are used to send fingerprints, bank documents, weather maps, X-ray photos, and photographs over wire or radio. Amateurs, too, can send photographs over such equipment.

Amateur radio is fun for the variety, the excitement, and the contacts it offers. But the hobby takes a giant leap beyond pure enjoyment. Many nonhams are not even aware of the services amateurs provide to the community, and to the world. Some of these services deal with life-and-death situations.

CHAPTER SIX

THE SERVICE OF AMATEUR RADIO

Through uncountable emergencies, hams have acted to assist where needed. The narrative below will give you a taste of amateur work. It is part of an actual ham broadcast taped during a tornado emergency in Alabama.

Radio announcer: 24C tornado warning. Tornado warning issued 3:55 p.m. CST, Jan. 10. . . . Tornadoes are moving toward the northeast some 50 to 60 miles [80–97 km] per hour.

Miles away in the stricken area of Alabama, amateur radio operator Hop Hayes broadcasts from his truck.

Hop: We got damage. I mean off of Chapel Lane. . . . We do have damage right here.

Radio control:	How far did it go?
Hop:	My God, I'm in the middle of it right now. . . . I got trees down all around me now. I'm going to get out of this truck. It's about to turn my truck over. [Pause] It looks like we might've had some damage to the power down here. . . . Oh, no. I think we're going to have another one. Here comes.
Radio control:	Go ahead, Hop. All stations, all frequencies, please stand by. Leave your power to emergency communications.
Hop:	I don't know what it's got in it, but it's getting ready to come back across the same place right now. We're getting some hail and heavy rains. . . .

HELPING PEOPLE

Emergency assistance is one important service performed by amateur operators. It is life and death work, as Hop Hayes can tell you.

Ask Mark Baretella, too, who was on Grenada when it was invaded in 1983. At risk to his life, Mark stuck to his radio, linking his Grenadian student friends and their families at home. His was the only news that left Grenada for several days.

Through floods, hurricanes, blizzards, fires, earthquakes, mine cave-ins, commercial power failures, air crashes, shipwrecks, hams have often saved lives because of their radio work. Theirs is a faceless heroism.

Even at that, there need not be wholesale disaster for hams to be on the job.

When a young boy in isolated Lazy Bay, Alaska, developed appendicitis, a Seattle ham picked up the message for help and a doctor gave a 2,000-mile (3,220-km) diagnosis. Another message was beamed to Anchorage, where a plane was sent to pick up the boy.

A South American ham sent out a call to locate a special garment for burn victims. A United States amateur heard the call and put the South American ham in touch with a specialist who could help. A garment was eventually sent.

Besides emergencies, there is the message service hams provide. When weather reports were needed for the Olympic Torch Run from Virginia to Lake Placid for the 1980 winter games, hams provided the service. Every year amateurs send messages to Santa Claus from hospitalized children at Christmas and assist family members in contacting mothers on Mother's Day.

Hams, too, have a civilian connection with the military forces through the Military Affiliate Radio System (MARS). In addition to acting as a trained force in case of emergency, hams associated with MARS provide a radio contact link between military personnel anyplace in the world and their families back home.

Through past years, ham radios have gone along on famous expeditions as well. They have traveled to the Amazon, the Arctic Circle, Greenland, Antarctica, the Sahara Desert, the West Indies, Tibet, and the Andes. Besides regular transportation, amateur radio has signaled from yachts, dog sleds, dirigibles, whaling boats, and submarines. And of course from the space shuttle *Columbia.*

Hams are of service to the military and to people all over the globe. Not surprisingly then, they are also interested in people with special problems or handicaps. The blind and the deaf/blind, in particular, have benefited from amateur radio.

Bob Gunderson is a case in point. He is not only a traveler, film producer, and author, but has taught blind students, and designed special electrical equipment himself. Blind from birth, Gunderson found ham radio early and has since shared his hobby with other blind or deaf/blind students.

How, you might ask, can a blind or deaf/blind person learn all the radio theory and rules without seeing or hearing?

For blind students, Bob uses speech, touch, and sound to get his teaching across. For the deaf/blind, he "speaks" braille onto their hands with his fingers and then uses strong vibrations—sometimes through headphones—for the actual radio practice.

For blind and deaf people, the process of learning ham is a painful and frustrating one. It takes patience, but the rewards are worth it. For some, it broadens their circle of friends to include the entire world.

ALWAYS TRYING SOMETHING NEW: THE EXPERIMENTERS

Whether learning radio by vibration or by experimentation, challenge seems the key. A number of amateurs would rather fiddle with transistors or test things with a computer than rag-chew over the air. That is why hams have led the way to scientific answers.

With amateur radio reaching into space, the moon is the target of experimenters. Very high (VHF) and ultrahigh (UHF) frequencies travel by line of sight. If you can see it, a radio signal can go there. Bouncing signals off the moon is called EME, which is a short way of saying "earth-moon-earth," or "*moonbounce.*" First accomplished in 1960, moonbounce is somewhat different from *OSCAR*, in that the moon provides a fairly fixed target.

But because the moon is so far away, the radio signal must be extremely strong to reach that far. Amateurs must use very large dish antennas in order to send out a signal strong enough. And the radio beam must have rifle-sure accuracy.

Not only that, but the earth and moon must be in the right position. That way the signal can bounce off the moon and then reach a certain, targeted spot on earth. There are some amateurs who enjoy juggling the factors in spite of the problems involved.

In 1976, Dr. Allen Katz was the first amateur to receive a WAC (Worked All Continents) award through moonbounce. The doctor started his ham career by obtaining a Novice license at the age of twelve. Always experimenting, he was determined to reach all continents with the signal reflected off the moon.

Besides the technical problems, Katz had a special one. After working all continents except one, he found there was no moonbounce ham in South America to receive his signal. As a result, other amateurs interested in EME sent an expedition to Colombia, South America. There they set up a station so Katz's signal could be received by way of the moon. When the scheduled time arrived, the adventurers at the Colombian site had to actually hold up the enormous portable antenna by their hands in order to correct for the wind. Thus, properly pointed, the moonbounce was completed.

Sometimes the doctor has trouble at home with his outside equipment. You might think the problem is wind or rain which could blow down his antenna, or maybe that the atmosphere is playing tricks and his signals cannot get through. But no—one of

Dr. Allen Katz adjusts the huge antenna near his home. The antenna is a vital element in completing moonbounce contacts.

the problems outside his house is a down-to-earth one. It is ground squirrels who chew through his antenna cables.

A major problem with experimenting is that often there are no instruments available to do the necessary job. Amateurs do not let that stop them. They just go ahead and design their own tools. That, too, is how further discoveries are made.

With moonbounce and *OSCAR*, you might wonder where hams will go next. Actually there is an amateur, right now, who is trying to bounce signals off the planet Venus. There is no limit to an experimenter's imagination.

——————— DEVELOPING WORLD FRIENDSHIPS ———————

Radio beams might reach far into space, but it is a human here on earth who sends the signal.

No matter where on the globe, people agree that hobbies are developed because of personal interests. Race, nationality, or politics do not enter in. Just as radio waves know no boundaries, so it is true with amateur operators. The friendship of hams all over the world ties the hobby together. It is a bond which rises above the rivalry of countries and acts as a handshake between nations. Amateur radio operators—hams—are true ambassadors of the airways.

GLOSSARY

Amateur—a person who follows a pursuit as a hobby rather than as a calling or a paying job. In radio he or she is a licensed operator, also known as a "ham."

Amplification—the process of making sound and radio waves stronger.

Amplitude—the height (the largest or peak value) of a radio wave measured from zero.

Antenna—an electrical conductor attached to a transmitter and receiver used to send or receive radio waves.

Apogee—the farthest or highest point from a planet reached by an object orbiting it. The nearest point is called the perigee.

Atom—one of the smallest particles of any chemical matter in our universe. Atoms are made up of particles such as electrons, protons, and neutrons and are the source of vast potential energy.

Autopatch—the process of connecting a radio repeater station with the local telephone system.

Band—the range of frequencies on the radio spectrum between two particular limits. For instance, a normal broadcast band covers from 550 to 1,600 kilocycles.

Channel—the band of frequencies wide enough for one radio or TV transmission. Transmissions are kept within a channel to prevent interference with stations on other nearby channels.

Crest—the high point, or peak, of a radio wave. The low point of the wave is called the trough.

Cycle—one complete up-and-down motion of an electromagnetic wave. In radio it is also called a hertz.

Downlink—a radio frequency signal beaming downward from a satellite to earth after the original earth frequency signal (uplink) has been received and converted by the satellite.

Electromagnetic wave—a vibration made by varying electric and magnetic forces. All such waves travel at the speed of light, which is itself electromagnetic waves.

Electron—one of the smallest, most basic units of negative electricity, and part of the atom. A positive unit is called a proton.

Elliptical—of, relating to, or shaped like an ellipse; an elongated circle, similar to an oval in shape.

Facsimile—the sending of graphic material such as photographs or signatures by radio waves, and their reproduction.

Frequency—the number of cycles of electromagnetic waves in one second.

Generator—a machine that changes mechanical energy to electric energy.

Ham—a familiar name for a licensed amateur radio operator.

Handie-talkie—a hand-held, frequency-modulated radio.

Hertz—one complete up-and-down motion of a radio wave, also called a cycle.

Ionosphere—the layers of electrically charged gases which surround the earth at a height of from 50 to 250 miles (80–402 km).

Kilocycles—a unit of metric measure meaning 1,000 cycles. In radio, it can also be written kilohertz (kHz).

Megacycles—a unit of metric measure meaning 1,000,000 cycles. In radio, it can also be written megahertz (MHz).

Meteor scatter—a shower of electric particles produced when meteors enter the earth's atmosphere and are burned up by friction.

Modulate—the process of mixing audio frequency energy from a microphone with a radio frequency wave that is going to carry it.

Moonbounce—the method of sending a radio message into space, having the signal reflect from the moon, and then receiving it on earth. Another name for this activity is earth-moon-earth, or EME.

Morse code—a system of code using long or short bursts of sound to send messages.

Propagation—the travel of electromagnetic waves through a medium, such as the earth's atmosphere.

Proton—one of the smallest, most basic units of positive electricity, and part of the atom. The negative unit is called an electron.

Receiver—part of a radio set which changes electric waves into sound signals.

Relay—the act of passing messages along by stages, one after another.

Repeater—an automatic radio station that receives and resends a signal, extending its range.

Scanner—a receiver that automatically looks for an open, or live, channel.

Sidebands—the band of frequencies on either side of a carrier frequency produced by amplitude modulation.

Spectrum—an arrangement of elements according to some kind of varying characteristic. For example, the radio spectrum is arranged according to the length of radio waves, from the longest along the spectrum to the shortest.

Sunspots—dark regions on the surface of the sun.

Transceiver—a unit combining a receiver and a transmitter in one cabinet and sharing controls.

Transistor—a small device that amplifies or adjusts electrical impulses.

Transmitter—an item of radio equipment that produces a radio carrier signal, modulates this carrier with information, and sends it into space.

Transponder—a radio set that receives a designated signal and then sends a signal of its own.

Trough—the lowest point of a radio wave cycle. The highest point is called the crest.

Uplink—a radio frequency signal beaming up from earth to a satellite.

Wavelength—the distance traveled by a radio wave in a time of 1 cycle, or 1 hertz.

Wireless—having no wire or wires; another name for a radio set.

TO LEARN MORE ABOUT
AMATEUR RADIO

———————————— FURTHER READING ——————————

Bendick, Jeanne, and Lefkowitz, R.J. *Electronics for young People.* New York: McGraw-Hill, 1973.

Berger, Melvin. *Computers in Your Life.* New York: Thomas Y. Crowell, 1981.

Branley, Franklyn M. *Colombia and Beyond.* New York: William Collins, 1979.

Gunston, David. *Marconi.* New York: Crowell-Collier Press, 1965.

Luciani, Vince. *Amateur Radio, Super Hobby!* New York: McGraw-Hill, 1984.

Weiss, Ann E. *Tune In, Tune Out.* Boston: Houghton-Mifflin, 1981.

The American Radio Relay League, Inc.
225 Main Street
Newington, CT 06111

AMSAT
Radio Amateur Satellite Corp.
P.O. Box 27
Washington, DC 20044

Federal Communications Commission
1919 M. Street, N.W.
Washington, DC 20554

Canadian Radio Relay League
Box 7009
Station E
London, Ontario, Canada N5Y 4J9

Information can also be obtained by consulting ham magazines, many of which are found in local libraries, on newsstands, or in stores that sell ham equipment. Such magazines include the following:

QST Magazine
73 Magazine
CQ Magazine
Ham Radio Magazine
Worldradio Newspaper

INDEX

Advanced license, 31, 33
Airplanes, 15
Alaska earthquake, 7–8, 44
Alsbury, Jim, 34
Amateur Extra license, 31, 33
American Radio Relay League (ARRL), 14,
    30, 31, 36, 51, 69
Amplification, 15
Amplifiers, 23
Amplitude, 24
AMSAT (Radio Amateur Satellite Corpora-
    tion), 51, 69
Antennas, 23, 27–28, 33, 47, 52
Apogee, 52
Armstrong, Edwin, 15
ASCII (American Standard Code for Informa-
    tion Interchange), 47
Atmosphere, radio wave behavior in, 40, 42
Atoms, 18
Autopatch, 48–49
Awards, 36–37

Baker, Dean, 38
Bands, 16
Baretella, Mark, 58

Bell, Dave, 40, 54
Blind hams, 60

Call signs, 35–36
Canadian Radio Relay League, 69
Channels, 16
Citizens band (CB) radio, 30–31
Clubs, 30, 43–44
Columbia space shuttle, 48, 59
Commercial radio broadcasting, 16
Computers, 46, 47
Conrad, Frank, 16
Continuous wave transmission (CW), 45–46,
    49
CQ, 35, 36
Crest, 19, 26
Crippen, Dr. Hawley, 13
Cycles, 22, 26

De Forest, Lee, 12–13
Deaf hams, 60
Delay, 16
Directional antennas, 29
Downlink, 49
DXCC (DX Century Club) certificate, 36

DXpeditions, 39–43, 54

Earphones, 15
Electricity, 11, 19, 24, 31
Electromagnetic waves, 19, 24
Electrons, 17, 18
Elliptical orbit, 52
EME (earth-moon-earth), 61–63
Emergency assistance, 7–8, 38, 44, 57–59

Facsimile (FAX), 56
Faraday, Michael, 11
Fast-scan television (ATV), 55–56
Federal Communications Commission
    (FCC), 16, 31–32, 69
Field Day, 43–44
Fleming, John, 12
Frequency, 16, 24–26
Frequency modulation (FM), 25

Garriott, Owen, 48
General license, 31, 32–33, 53
Generators, 44
Giugliano, Tom, 32
Going mobile, 43
Goldwater, Barry, 31
Ground waves, 27
Gunderson, Bob, 60

Hams:
    characteristics of, 9
    defined, 8
Ham shack, 8, 33
Hamfests, 44
Handie-talkie, 26, 47–48
Hayes, Hop, 57–58
Hernandez, John, 34
Hertz, 22, 26
Hertz, Heinrich, 11, 22
Holliday, Lynn, 34
Hopewell, Gary, 34

Information sources, 69
International Telecommunications Union, 16
Ionosphere, 15–16, 27, 40, 42

Katz, Allen, 61, 62
Kilocycles, 22
Kilohertz (kHz), 22

Language, 37–38
Licenses, 14, 30–33
"Line of sight" waves, 27
Lisle, Larry, 34

Macdonald, Cop, 53, 54
Magazines, 69
Magnetism, 19
Marconi, Guglielmo, 10–12, 17
Maritime Mobile Nets, 38
Maxwell, James Clerk, 11
Megacycles, 22
Megahertz (MHz), 22
Meteor scatters, 42
"Mickey Mouse Nets," 38
Microwaves, 19
Military Affiliate Radio System (MARS), 59
Mitchell, Guy, 31
Modulates, 24
Moonbounce, 61–63
Morse, Samuel, 45
Morse code, 10, 31, 32, 37, 45–46

National Aeronautics and Space Administra-
    tion (NASA), 51, 52
Navassa Island, 39
Neal, Roy, 48
Novice license, 31–32

OSCAR (Orbiting Satellite Carrying Amateur
    Radio), 36, 49, 50–52, 61, 63

PACSAT (packet radio satellite), 52
Phillips, Jack, 13
Propagation, 42, 52
Protons, 18

Q codes, 37–38
QSL cards, 36

Radio Act of 1912, 14

Radio waves, 18–29
Rag Chewers certificate, 37
Receivers, 23, 33
Reinartz, 16
Relay, 38
Repeaters, 48–49
RTTY, 46–47

Satellites, 27, 29, 36, 49, 51–52, 61, 63
Scanners, 47
Schaefer, Kristine, 34
Schnell, 16
Ships at sea, 13
Shortwaves, 15–16, 27
Sidebands, 24
Signal Hill, St. John's, Newfoundland, 10, 12
Single sideband transmission (SSB), 24, 49
Slow-scan television (SSTV), 53–56
Soundwaves, 22–24
Spectrum, radio, 16
Station, setting up, 33
Sunspots, 42

Technician license, 31, 32
Television, 27, 53, 55–56

Titanic, 13
Transatlantic wireless experiment, first, 10–12
Transceivers, 43
Transistors, 24
Transmission, 24–25
Transmitters, 23, 33
Transponders, 49
Trough, 19, 26

Ultrahigh (UHF) frequency, 60
U.S. Signal Corps, 14–15
Upchurch, Chris, 34
Uplink, 49

Venus, 63
Very high (VHF) frequency, 27, 29, 60

WAC (Worked All Continents), 36, 61
WAS (Worked All States), 36
Wavelengths, 14, 15, 26–27
Wireless, 10–13
World Administrative Radio Conferences, 16
World friendships, 63
World War I, 14–15